Heart Rhymes

Poems During the National Poetry Writing
Month, April 2021

Saurav Banerjee

ISBN 978-93-5458-777-1

© Saurav Banerjee 2021

Published in India 2021 by Pencil

A brand of

One Point Six Technologies Pvt. Ltd.

123, Building J2, Shram Seva Premises,

Wadala Truck Terminal, Wadala (E)

Mumbai 400037, Maharashtra, INDIA

E connect@thepencilapp.com

W www.thepencilapp.com

DISCLAIMER: *The opinions expressed in this book are those of the authors and do not purport to reflect the views of the Publisher.*

Author biography

Hailing from Aligarh, UP, India, Saurav Banerjee is pursuing his graduation (BA) from reputed Shri Varshney Degree College, in Aligarh itself.

Apart from his studies, he is following his passion of writing, has published his four books, and also has co-authored a few anthologies. He also writes quotes, poems, etc. on the YourQuote App, since September, 2017.

CONTENTS

Introduction

Heart Rhymes is a collection of poems author wrote during the National Poetry Writing Month, i.e. April, 2021.

Poem 1 - About You (01 April, 2021)

They ask me about you.

For them You're new.

They ask, "who's she, for whom you write?"

My poems on you make them excite.

I guess, they've created their own funny assumption.

They think I'm in love, with Mysterious Someone.

Poem 2 - Rooftop (02 April, 2021)

On my rooftop,

I stare the sky with full of hope.

I think of this city which is lacking in scope.

Difficulties are on the way, vague how to cope.

Poem 3 - Clueless Mind (03 April, 2021)

I sat down to write a poem,

But the topic is unknown.

Clueless on what to write,

Something fictional, or past's plight?

My mind is running out of content.

in thwe search of the same, half-an-hour I spent.

Poem 4 - Conversational Poem (04 April, 2021)

"Ma'am, I've done something wrong. Will you forgive me?" asked a child.

"It's completely okay doing the things wrong, my dear," ma'am replied.

"By the way, what wrong you've done?" ma'am asked further.

"I've told one lie to you, I shouldn't," child replied, still in fear.

"Relax, my child, you must felt its need so you lied. And it's fine," ma'am pacified.

"Thank you, ma'am. I'm grateful to you," child expressed gratitude, feeling light.

Poem 5 - My Reverse Poem (05 April, 2021)

Writer.

Is a fighter,

Who fights using words

Sharper than the swords.

READ IT BACKWARDS

Poem 6 - Today's Evening (06 April, 2021)

The air is warmer than before,

I'm getting nervous a bit more.

Uncertain what'll happen in the evening today,

As a presentation & speech is scheduled to display.

Though I've enoug time till evening,

But still, quite worried am feeling.

Poem 7 - A College Department (07 April, 2021)

There's a department in college, I hesitate to go there.

Some reasons for the same I can't share.

Though there's nothing wrong with the department,

But still I feel a bit awkward, so i keep distant.

Due to the necessity to go one day every week, I force myself.

Unwillingly I attend the class, I couldn't help.

Poem 8 - Meme Makers (08 April, 2021)

Being a meme maker isn't cool as it seems,

People often judge them without knowing what's behind the scenes.

"Memers are mannerless," some people say.

But still they try to make people laugh whole day.

People rarely appreciates the efforts, even if the memes made them laugh.

It's what sometimes make memers sad, I wrote this poem on their behalf.

Poem 9 - Necessary Imperfections (09 April, 2021)

In the search of perfection, don't doubt yourself.

If there are imperfections in you, don't shout on yourself.

Let your imperfections be with you,

Because it's important to have a few.

It's your imperferctions that make you unique,

To having imperfections doesn't mean you're weak.

In the imperfections only you'll find the artistic beauty,

Where there's imperfection, there'll be literature and creativity.

Poem10 - The Lost Self (10 April, 2021)

Yesterday, I was going through an old album,

Photos in it were saying very happy I am.

I wondeered looking my own photos of childhood,

Wish if my childhoodwas still here, if it could.

It seemed I never faked my smile when I was a child,

Now that child is lost, and that smile, somehow almost died.

Poem 11 - Found A Way to You (11 April, 2021)

I found my way back to you,

In the passion of writing I pursue.

I meet you in memories often,

And write some poems then.

There was a time no one believed me, only you did.

You were always with me even when I didn't need.

Don't know if we'll ever meet again in real,

But whenever I remember you, happy I feel.

Poem 12 - Facts About George Bernard Shaw (12 April, 2021)

Let's talk about some facts on GB Shaw,

I wrote them down here as I saw.

On 26th July, 1856 george Bernard Shaw was born,

By Bernard Shaw he is also known.

He began his literary career with the novel

Immaturity in 1879,

But failed to find a publisher at that time.

Then one-by-one 52 years gone,

Immaturity published in 1931.

By 1900 it came his fruitful days,

When he was an established playwright with 63 plays.

"Saint Joan," and "Heartbreak House" are the two of

his notable works he did write,

And on 2nd of November, 1950 he died.

Poem 13 - About A Test (13 April, 2021)

That dayn is here,

There'll be a test I need to clear.

Though I'm not afraid,

I just need to give my best.

There are a few things I'm thinking about,

Will i be able to meet my own expectations, a bit I doubt.

Not only expectations, somen other things are also interlinked with it.

While thinking all these, sometimes I feel like a nit.

Poem 14 - My LMAO Dream (14 April, 2021)

Every night I dream, like anything.

Sometimes weird they seem.

Yesterday, in dream, my ex-crush did text me.

"You're my crush," texted she.

In that dream only, wondered reading that text,.

It seemed like dream was also on weed, I guess.

I LOLed my self after waking up,

After many dsys it happened my dream made me laugh.

Poem 15 - Love Walks Away (15 April, 2021)

Love walks away,

When alterations succeed to nake its way.

It feels awkward then,

When changes are there all of a sudden.

That time Love feels the pain,

It tries to explain, but often fails in the same.

It happens either when the love is not true,

Or whan it's being judged as fake or untrue.

Poem 16 - How to Fix a Heart (16 April, 2021)

Talk with it, say it to rest.

Convince it to not compare, it's at its best.

Tell it, "it's okay to be slow,

Please don't you hurry, bro."

It's your very own heart, it needs your love.

Whenever it feels sad, do anything to make it laugh.

When it starts getting worried, make it calm down.

Love it more, appreciate it enough, just don't let it feel like drawn.

Poem 17 - An Odd Numbered Poem (17 April, 2021)

Sitting in my room, with my shadow.

It never leaves me, my only fellow.

Never talks, unlike I do.

It's black in clolour, but it's true.

It's my identical, 'cause together we grew.

Poem 18 - Tomorrow's Suspense (18 April, 2021)

Tomorrow is a suspense,

It'll be a bit draining for me, I sense.

A part of my daiy routine is goimg to end,

Following that routine more than one year I spent.

Enjoyed every offline days in this routine,

Now what will I do after this, I'm thinkin'.

I have created some memories as well,

In those memories sometimes my mind will dwell.

Poem 19 - Feeling-less (19 April, 2021)

I don't know how am feeling, good or bad.

I'm somewhere in the middle, happy and sad.

Shoiuld I feel excited, or should I feel cheerless?

My feelings right now is feeling-less.

Untill yesterday I was excited for today,

Now that excitement is far away.

A group of people will sayu goodbye to each other,

Will they meet ever again? Might be never.

Poem 20 - Roots of Sadness (20 April, 2021)

Roots of sadness grow,

When we try to please everyone we know.

We try to meet others' expectations on us,

And when we fail we create a fuss.

Stop doing this, it's the need of time.

Trust me, to not meet people's expectations is fine.

It's okay if they think you arwe not good,

Let them, if they have missunderstood.

Poem 21 - Market of Memories (21 April, 2021)

In the market of memories,

I can spend a good amount of time with ease.

I never get bored there,

'Cause there is stillI am with my friends together.

We are still kid doing fun,

Or bragging about a game in past we won.

Those werwe the days we realy did enjoy,

Now worries are more, and lesse is the joy.

Poem 22 - My 2nd Year's Thursdays in the College (22 April, 2021)

Thusdaus are not going interesting in the college,

There this day I feel awkward in some ways.

Every week this days I say to myself,

"Fuck, yaar! You now have to attend thagt class,

could not help thyself."

Unwillingly I attend that class one day every week,

In that class I don't feel at ease, as I seek.

I seriusy want t bunk that class,

But than I think its internal marks will help me to pass.

Poem 23 - Heavy Emotions (23 April, 2021)

Sometimes I feel heavy inside,

Maybe due to the emotions I mostly hide.

I behave formal to hide it all inside me,

Avoid making eye contact so that they can't sense or see.

I giggle, I laugh, often I fake my smile,

By this way I usually suceed, thay think it's my style.

Anyway, what to do when there is no one to share?

So I prefer to hide emotions, 'cause no one cares.

Poem 24 - Leave, If You Wish (24 April, 2021)

Don't wait for me,

If you want to lweave, you are free.

Don't worry for me, I will manage without you,

I am habitual of living alone, for mr it is not new.

You are free to stay or leave,

Don't think of me of how will I live.

Know if you are hgappy, I am fine.

Leave me if you wish, don't waste your time.

Poem 25 - Small Words (25 April, 2021)

With small words,

I sometimes write about our that childhood world.

Those childish things and innocent lies,

These are the moments I still memorize.

Poem 26 - Lack of Bond (26 April, 2021)

There are many people I know,

Mostly are elder than me, though,

But am not having bond with all of them,

I also not tried much to create the same.

There are very less people to whom I am a bit frank,

Or to the rest either talk formally, or go blank.

I usually sit quiet, often alone, and observe.

So to the some people, I look weird and reserve.

Poem 27 - Hold My Hand (27 April, 2021)

Hold my hand like I am about to drown.

Hold my hand like as if to never withdraw.

Hold my hand like as I am the only one you know.

Hold my hand like as if to walk along.

Hold my hand like a if to relive the past that is gone.

Poem 28 - An Observed Hug (28 April 2021)

I recall a memory not so old,

For me very importance it holds.

It was one of the old days of a subject's syllabus,

In class for unknown reasons a student was looking sad between us.

I was sitting on the backbench so didn't notice it at first,

It was when the teacher recognised it and did assert.

Teacher called that sudent when the period was o'er,

Student was worrierd about exams and was having some fear.

Student foumd the solace in the teacher, and the

worries were no more there,

After being hugged and consoled. That hug worked as a pacifier.

Poem 29 - I Did Backspace (29 April, 2021)

Many things in my mind I say,

Before xending someone a text.

I wrote them too, and then I thought,

"Should I send this exact? Um... No, I should not."

In that text visible the emotions,

So I required to do a few modifications.

I did backspace and edited that text a good few times,

And sent when the emotions were less, and it seemed fine.

Poem 30 - I Felt What You Said In My Dream (30 April, 2021)

I fremember what you said in my dream one day,

"Distance won't affect our friendship," you did say.

"I miss your friendship sometimes," I then said.

"I will be invisibly there, you will feel whenever you need," you further added.

I was missing you yesterday also, wished if you were here.

Got goosebumps when suddenly a storm came from nowhere.

If it was a coincidence or not, is yet not clear.

I felt it was you in the form of storm came to me, my dear.